Maggot

Paul Jennings

Stanley Thornes (Publishers) Ltd

© Paul Jennings 1986

All rights reserved. No part of this publication may be reproduced or transmitted in any form or by any means, electronic or mechanical, including photocopy, recording, or any information storage and retrieval system, without permission in writing from the publisher or under licence from the Copyright Licensing Agency Limited. Further details of such licences (for reprographic reproduction) may be obtained from the Copyright Licensing Agency Limited, of 90 Tottenham Court Road, London W1P 9HE.

First published in 1986 by Hutchinson Education

Reprinted 1992 by
Stanley Thornes (Publishers) Ltd
Ellenborough House
Wellington Street
CHELTENHAM GL50 1YW
England

98 99 00 / 10 9 8

British Library Cataloguing in Publication Data

Jennings, Paul
  Maggot. — (Spirals).
  1. Readers for new literates
  I. Title II. Series
  428.6'2   PE1126.A4

ISBN 0 7487 1041 8

Cover photograph by Steve Richards.
Cover design by Ned Hoste
Printed and bound in Great Britain at Martin's The Printers, Berwick.

1

I am writing this from jail. From a small cell which has bars on the window, a hard wooden bed, a small desk and a bucket. And a locked door.

The food is terrible. Thin soup and bread and a small bit of meat. Water to drink. How I wish for a nice piece of steak and a pot of beer!

There is no one to talk to. I am on my own. Isolated. There is nothing much to do. Time passes slowly. Life is boring. That's why I'm writing my story.

Once a day I'm allowed to go outside. The screws put me into a small yard. It has high walls all around it. I'm supposed to run or jog. This is my only chance to exercise.

The exercise yard has no trees or flowers. It's bare and flat. It's a long time since I've seen grass or plants. Or a girl.

None of the other prisoners are allowed near me. The screws say that I'm dangerous. That I would escape if I could. They're right. I'll get out of here one day.

I shouldn't be in jail. I have done nothing wrong. I'm innocent. One day I'll pay everyone back. I'll have my revenge.

2

It all started with a smell. A bad smell. Something was causing a big stink in my kitchen. It was like rotten eggs. Only worse.

I looked everywhere but I could not find what was making the smell. I looked in all of the cupboards and behind the fridge. I looked under the sink and in the pantry.

It was driving me crazy. Every day it got worse. It became so bad that I couldn't eat in my own kitchen. I had to go out and have dinner at the pub.

My friends wouldn't visit me because the smell was so awful.

I had to do something about it or I would have to move out and find another home.

One day I noticed that the smell was worse near the kitchen door. I sniffed around a lot but couldn't see anything. The only thing there was the light switch. The smell seemed to be coming from the light switch.

I fetched a screwdriver from the toolshed. I took off

the light switch cover. Sitting up in the wall was a dead mouse.

Would you believe it? A dead mouse. All that smell from one tiny mouse. It must have touched the wires and got an electric shock.

I pulled out the mouse and went to throw it in the bin. I couldn't. I wanted to throw that mouse in the bin but something was stopping me.

I told my feet to go to the rubbish bin. They took me over to the table instead. I wanted to throw that dead mouse out but I couldn't. It had some sort of power over me. I put the rotten, smelly mouse on the table and left it there.

3

I went and lay down on my bed. I felt silly. Why had I left the mouse there? Why couldn't I throw it out? I had put it on the kitchen table. What a stupid thing to do.

I tried not to think about it. I closed my eyes, trying to shut it out.

It was no use. I couldn't stop thinking about that mouse. It seemed to be calling me. Inside my head a voice was calling me. Pulling me towards the kitchen.

I went back to the kitchen and had another look at it. What I saw made me ill. I rushed into the bathroom and was sick.

A large maggot was eating the mouse. It was curled up in the eye socket. I had never seen such a big maggot before.

This time I wasn't going to fool around. I picked up a brush and pan. I was going to throw that mouse out. When I tried to sweep up the mouse I felt a sharp pain in my head. It was like an electric current in my head. I screamed out and dropped the brush and pan.

The pain stopped at once. I went up to the mouse and looked at it closely. The maggot was white and fat. It was about the size of a small caterpillar. It had no legs or eyes.

It was hungry. It had finished eating the mouse and wanted something else. I knew that it wanted food. Somehow I knew that it wanted food. It wanted cheese. It was telling me that it wanted cheese.

A voice in my head was telling me to get cheese.

'No way,' I said. 'I'm not getting food for a maggot.'

The pain came back into my head. It hurt like hell. It was unbearable.

'OK, OK,' I shouted. 'I'll get cheese.'

I went over to the fridge and got some cheese. I put it on to the table next to the mouse. The maggot wiggled on to the table and over to the cheese. It ate a little hole into the cheese. I couldn't see it any more. It had disappeared into the cheese.

I jumped into bed with my clothes on. Maybe this was all a bad dream. A nightmare. I hoped that I would wake up and see nothing. No mouse, no cheese and no maggot.

4

I got one of my wishes. In the morning there was no cheese. The skeleton of the mouse was still there and so was the maggot. It had grown fat. It had eaten a whole slab of cheese in one night.

It made me feel sick to look at it. The maggot had grown as big as my thumb. It was white and shiny and wet. It looked revolting.

I thought about throwing it out for the birds to eat. My head started to throb. The maggot was telling me not to try it. There was nothing I could do to hurt this maggot.

A picture came into my head. It was a picture of food. It wanted more to eat. Meat. It wanted meat.

I knew that if I didn't fetch meat I'd get another electric shock in my head. I went to the fridge and got out a chop. A lovely juicy chop. I was keeping this chop for my tea. I did not want to give my tea to a revolting looking maggot. But I had no choice.

I put the chop next to the maggot. It wriggled over to it and then stopped. It seemed to be looking at me. My head began to hurt. It hurt a lot.

'Stop it,' I screamed. 'What more do you want? You've got my tea. Isn't it good enough for you?'

It didn't want the chop. It wanted meat but it didn't want the chop.

The pain in my head became worse. It was telling me something. It was telling me to go outside. I was glad to go outside. I wanted to get away from the smell of the dead mouse and the sight of a live maggot.

My feet walked towards my car. The maggot was forcing me into my car. I drove down the street to town. My hands and feet made me go. The pain in my head made me go. A maggot was forcing me to drive my car into town.

I thought that I must be going to the butcher to get meat. The maggot probably wanted rump steak. A chop wasn't good enough for it. It was sending me to the butcher for something better.

I was wrong. The maggot wanted me to read a book. It made me stop at the library.

I thought that I might be able to run away and escape. After all the maggot was at home on the kitchen table. Two miles away.

As soon as I thought this I received a bad shock of pain in my head. The maggot knew what I was thinking. There was no escape.

I went into the library and borrowed a book about insects. The maggot wanted me to read this book. It made me turn to a page about flies. Blow flies. I read a whole chapter about blow flies.

The maggot was going to turn into a blow fly.

5

I learned a lot about blow flies. I learned that one fly can lay a thousand eggs. These eggs are laid on dead animals. They hatch out into maggots. The maggots eat the dead flesh.

Now I had found out why the maggot wanted me to read the book. Maggots only eat bad meat. They don't like fresh meat. They like rotten meat. Meat that is old and smells.

The maggot didn't like my chop because it was fresh. It wanted me to find some rotten meat. My head started to ache badly. The maggot was telling me to find some bad meat for it.

Where on earth could I find bad meat? No one wants bad meat. The butcher doesn't sell bad meat. It makes people sick.

The maggot was getting hungry. I could tell. The hungrier it got the more my head hurt. I had to find some rotten meat quickly. I couldn't stand the pain much longer.

I didn't know where to look for old meat. People throw it out. They don't keep it. That gave me an idea. They throw it out. Into rubbish bins.

I rushed out of the library. I looked untidy and dirty. I had slept in my clothes and I hadn't shaved.

I searched in a rubbish bin that was outside a shop. I dug around in the rubbish looking for old meat. There was none there.

People were starting to look at me. They must have thought that I was a drunk looking for food in the rubbish bins.

A lady came up to me. 'You poor man,' she said. 'Here's a pound for you to buy some food.'

She pushed the pound coin into my hand and rushed off. I felt silly. I was embarrassed.

I didn't like people looking at me. I decided to go behind the shops into a lane. This was where the shopkeepers threw their rubbish. No one would see me there.

I had to hurry. My head felt as if it was splitting open. The maggot wanted food.

There was nothing in the lane except a pile of rotten carrots and cabbages. The maggot needed meat, not vegetables.

Behind the pile of vegetables I saw something. A dead cat. The pain in my head was worse. The maggot wanted the dead cat.

I wasn't going to pick up a dead cat. Nothing was going to make me carry a dead cat down the street. Pain shot through my head. Terrible pain.

I picked up the cat by the tail. It was stiff as a board. And smelly. It stank.

I had to get back to my car. The maggot wouldn't let me put the cat down. It kept the pain going all the time.

I ran down the street with the cat. People were staring at me. I was unshaved and dressed in wrinkled clothes.

I didn't know what to do. I didn't have anything to carry the cat in. It had a foul smell. I didn't want people to see me carrying a dead cat. In the end I put it up my jumper. I put that stinking dead cat up my jumper.

I got home at last. I threw the dead cat on the table. The pain in my head stopped.

The maggot started to eat its meal.

6

I was a slave. A slave to a maggot. I had to get whatever it wanted. There was nothing I could do to escape. It knew what I was thinking.

While it was eating the dead cat I thought about getting a can of fly spray. I would kill it with fly spray. As soon as I had this thought the maggot gave me a terrible pain in the head. I fell to the ground, holding my face in my hands. I yelled out. 'Stop, stop. Please stop.'

The pain stopped at once. I didn't think about killing the maggot any more.

It was eating the cat quickly. By the end of the day it had finished. All that was left of the cat was bones. It was just a skeleton. In the kitchen was the skeleton of the mouse and the skeleton of the cat. The maggot had picked both skeletons clean. They were white and shiny.

The maggot had eaten its fill. And it had grown. It was as big as a rabbit. It was like a fat white sausage. It was shiny and wet. I felt ill just looking at it.

Tomorrow it would need more rotten meat. It sent me out to the butcher's shop. I bought a side of lamb. The lamb was so heavy that I could hardly carry it.

I put the lamb in the back yard. The maggot wanted the sun to shine on the meat to make it rot.

A little later there was a knock on the door. When I opened the door I saw two people. A policeman and a little old lady. The old lady was angry. She pointed a skinny finger at me and screeched out. 'That's him. That's him. He's the one who killed my cat. He killed Fluffy. I saw him running down the street. He put Fluffy up his jumper.'

'I am sorry, sir,' said the policeman. 'But this lady says that you killed her cat. Can we come in please?'

The maggot didn't want them to come in. By now I could tell what the maggot wanted before it hurt me.

'No,' I replied. 'You can't come in. I'm busy.'

The policeman started sniffing. 'What is that horrible smell? Something in here smells terrible.'

'A dead rat,' I lied. 'There's a dead rat in the ceiling.'

The whole house stank. The dead mouse, the dead cat and the maggot. They all stank to high heaven.

'You can't come in unless you have a search warrant. I didn't kill her cat. I have never seen her cat.' I shut the door in their faces. After a while they went away.

7

A week passed. By now the maggot was eating a whole side of beef every day. It had grown as big as a cow.

There were bones all over my house. I had to get rid of them. There was no room to move. I buried them in the back yard.

The smell was overpowering. The stink of rotten meat was everywhere. I had an old gas mask left over from the war. I had to wear it in the house. The maggot didn't seem to mind. I hadn't hurt its feelings. It wasn't offended.

The meat was very expensive. I was running out of money. I had very little left in the bank. The maggot was ruining me.

The butcher wanted to know what I was doing with all the meat. I was his best customer. He smiled every time I went into the shop.

'What do you want two hundred sausages for?' he asked one day.

'I've got a visitor,' I answered. 'A very hungry visitor.'

When I got back home with the sausages I found that the maggot had changed. It wasn't moving. Its skin had gone hard. It just lay in the corner of the kitchen.

I hoped that it was dead. Nothing happened to my head. No pain. I had a thought. I thought about kicking it. Nothing happened. Still no pain.

I went over and kicked it. It didn't move. It just lay there.

I was very happy. I jumped around. I danced around it. 'The maggot is dead. The maggot is dead,' I yelled. 'The stinking, rotten maggot is dead.'

I went over and looked at it carefully. My blood went cold. I got a terrible fright.

Inside the skin the maggot was changing. I could see two big eyes and wings. And legs. It was growing legs.

I remembered all the things that I had read about blow flies. I remembered that a maggot turns into a pupa. When it is a pupa it cannot move because it is changing. Changing into a blow fly.

It would be the biggest blow fly in the world. It would lay one thousand eggs. These eggs would hatch into one thousand maggots. The maggots would turn into blow flies and lay a thousand more eggs each. A million eggs.

A million blow flies making people get food for them. They might even kill or eat humans. They could rule the world. Blow flies the size of cars.

I was frightened. I was terrified. I had to stop the blow fly. I had to kill it while it was a pupa. It could not hurt my head while it was a pupa. I could do what I liked.

When it became a blow fly it might take revenge. It would know that I had kicked it.

I ran over to the cupboard and grabbed a can of fly spray. I sprayed it all over the pupa. It didn't work. I could see the blow fly inside the pupa skin starting to move. It was trying to get out. I must kill it while it was helpless.

I closed the kitchen door and locked it. Then I ran outside. I had to act fast. I piled up paper and sticks against the house and set fire to them.

It was a wooden house and it burned quickly. Soon the house was full of smoke. Flames were coming out of the roof.

I had a quick look through the kitchen window. The blow fly had come out of the pupa. It had large eyes and glinting wings. It was fanning its wings, trying to blow out the fire. It made a buzzing noise so loud that it hurt my ears.

As the fire became hotter the smoke grew thicker. Finally the blow fly fell over on to its back. It kicked its legs in the air, buzzing and spinning around in a circle. It hit the light on the ceiling and smashed it with its feet.

I had to leave the window. The fire was too hot. It drove me back.

The whole house was burning. Black smoke curled up into the sky. A fire engine arrived and a fireman began squirting a hosepipe on to the building. 'Stop,' I yelled. 'Let it burn, let it burn. There's a fly in there. A giant fly.'

The fireman didn't stop. He was trying to put out the fire. I ran up and punched him on the chin. Hard. He fell over and lay still.

Other firemen ran over and grabbed me. Someone hit me from behind. Everything went black.

When I woke up I was sitting in a police car. I was wearing handcuffs. The house had burned to the ground. The roof had fallen in. The fly was dead. Burned up. There was nothing left of it.

8

I have been in jail now for one year. I've been found guilty of three crimes. Killing a cat, hitting a fireman and burning down a house.

No one believes my story about a giant fly. They treat me like a crook. They say that I'm a dangerous criminal.

I saved the world. Flies would have been the rulers of the world if it weren't for me. People would have spent their lives under the control of giant flies.

The flies would have used pain to get what they wanted. They would have laid eggs and multiplied. They would have been the masters. Kings of the earth. I stopped all this happening.

What thanks do I get for my efforts? I'm put in jail. Locked up. Treated like a crazy man. No one is allowed near me. I'm kept in a cell all on my own in solitary confinement.

I'm going to get out. I'll escape and have revenge.

Every day they bring me food. I drink the soup and eat the bread. But I keep the little pieces of meat. I put them under my bed. They are starting to go bad. They smell a bit.

The screws can keep out visitors. But they can't keep out flies.

One piece of meat has maggots on it. One of the maggots is quite large.

He's a friendly little fellow. I'll do anything he wants.

Anything at all.

Anything . . .

Spirals Titles

Stories

Jim Alderson
Crash in the Jungle
The Witch Princess

Jan Carew
Death Comes to the Circus
Footprints in the Sand

Barbara Catchpole
Laura Called

Susan Duberley
The Ring

Keith Fletcher and Susan Duberley
Nightmare lake

John Goodwin
Ghost Train
Dead-end Job

Paul Groves
Not that I'm Work-shy

Anita Jackson
The Actor
The Austin Seven
Bennet Manor
Dreams
The Ear
A Game of Life or Death
No Rent to Pay

Paul Jennings
Eye of Evil
Maggot

Margaret Loxton
The Dark Shadow

Patrick Nobes
Ghost Writer

David Orme
The Haunted Asteroids
City of the Roborgs

Kevin Philbin
Summer of the Werewolf

John Townsend
Beware the Morris Minor
Fame and Fortune
SOS
Night Beast

Plays

Jan Carew
Computer Killer
No Entry
Time Loop

John Godfrey
When I Count to Three

Paul Groves
Tell Me Where it Hurts

Barbara Mitchelhill
Punchlines
The Ramsbottoms at Home

Julie Taylor
Spiders

John Townsend
Cheer and Groan
Hanging by a Fred
The Lighthouse Keeper's Secret
Making a Splash
Over and Out
Taking the Plunge
Breaking the Ice
Cowboys, Jelly and Custard
Spilling the Beans
Rocking the Boat
A Minute to Kill
A Bit of a Shambles

David Walke
The Good, the Bad and the Bungle
Package Holiday